Play With Y

Introduction

Chapter 1: Typical Early Feeding Development

Chapter 2: Tactile Sensory Processing

Chapter 3: Current Trends of Eating Skills

Chapter 4: Food Play Therapy

Chapter 5: Other Senses Involved in Eating

Chapter 6: Considerations for Children with Special Needs

Conclusion

References

## Introduction

Experiencing food by touching it is an important activity for all children with or without special needs. This becomes even more apparent every time I take my own children out to eat. When we eat at Mexican style restaurants, for example, if I order a taco for each of my children the waiter or waitress ALWAYS asks if they want "meat and cheese only?". My answer to this is always, "No, they want everything on it including lettuce and tomatoes". The waiter or waitress will then look very surprised, and usually comment on the fact that everyone else orders only meat and cheese on their kids' tacos. This may seem strange to people reading this since this is obviously a common way of ordering a simple taco. However, it seems very strange to me that 4 - 10 year-old kids aren't eating a taco as I know it with meat, cheese, lettuce, and tomatoes.

To me, this is one example of children who either have a limited diet, or are considered to be a picky eater. The reasons behind the "picky" eating can range from sensory based to behavioral based depending on each individual situation. As parents, we often make accommodations for our children especially when we go out to eat for the sake of getting through a meal without incidence. However, the ultimate goal or desire of all parents is to get through family meals without making any accommodations due to picky eating habits. In this book, I hope to educate parents on the importance of encouraging your children to play with their food so that one day, you might take your six year old out for a taco with everything on it.

I decided to write a book that explains the importance of allowing and encouraging children to play with their food because this topic comes up on a daily basis in my early intervention practice. In this book, I will explain why infants and toddlers go through certain developmental stages, and why it is important from a Tactile Sensory Processing point of view. Tactile Sensory Processing refers to the way our brains process or understand what we feel on our skin and inside our mouths. It is what most people would call one of our five senses: the Sense of Touch.

Of course, the point of this book is not actually to get all kids to eat tacos! This example is only a metaphor for the bigger goal for society. That goal is to educate parents on why and how the sense of touch is important in the development of eating skills for all kids. I hope this book will help parents so they can enjoy stress-free mealtimes with their family.

I have a Bachelor of Arts degree in Child Development (Human Development and Family Life) and a Bachelor of Science degree in Occupational Therapy. I have been working with families and children who have special needs in their home environment since 2001.

# Chapter 1: Typical Early Feeding Development

To begin, I would like to walk through the typical stages of feeding development beginning with infancy. As we all know, babies typically start out either taking a bottle with formula or breast milk, or nursing from their mother. Infants are born with a rooting reflex that helps them find their food. When you stimulate their cheek or mouth, they turn their head and face in that same direction to find the food source. Then, the sucking reflex helps them latch on to the nipple with their mouth and swallow the milk. There is a suck, swallow, breathe sequence that infants naturally follow in order to efficiently take in nourishment.

As infants grow, they begin to make eye contact with the person feeding them which establishes a trusting bond between baby and caregiver. Soon, the baby will begin to place their hand(s) on the bottle or breast while eating, and will eventually learn to hold a bottle independently. Some babies that are breast fed are never exposed to drinking from a bottle, but move directly to drinking from a cup when the time is right.

Once the infant reaches six months of age, they begin to take baby cereal from a spoon. Many parents start offering baby cereal earlier than this, however, most infants are not developmentally ready to eat from a spoon until at least six months. One way I advise parents to recognize when their child is old enough to eat from a spoon, is when they are able to sit independently. When a child is strong enough sit by themselves without falling over, it most likely means the muscles in their mouth and throat are also strong enough to safely swallow pureed foods. There are exceptions to this, so please consult your child's pediatrician or early intervention therapist for individualized recommendations.

When you begin to offer pureed foods, the "messy" eating phase begins. During mealtimes, you will end up getting at least some of the food on your baby's face around their mouth usually, and they will inevitably rub the food around with their hands. This often happens accidentally at first, and ultimately becomes a purposeful activity especially when the baby realizes that he or she can get even more of that food in their mouth by sucking on their messy hands. Here is the first step to self-feeding, or what I consider "finger feeding." Messy eating will continue as more baby foods are introduced. Not only will babies taste the food off their hands, but they will also play with the food on the high chair tray. This is a normal stage of feeding development. The baby is exploring new textures and flavors of baby foods in their mouth and on their hands at the same time.

This is a critical time in eating development for babies! Many parents will wipe the baby's face immediately after each bite offered, or be so careful they never get any on their face in the first place. Some parents go to great lengths to keep the high chair tray wiped even when a small amount of food might drop onto the tray during the meal. I can understand these actions in certain instances; for example, you are feeding the baby quickly because you have a doctor's appointment and you don't want them to be sticky and messy. Perhaps visitors are coming and you just don't have time to get the child in the bath before they arrive. Things like these are understandable. However, for the rest of the meals it is important to let the child get messy. Most of the time, they can be cleaned up with a wash rag. I often recommend that parents remove the child's clothing so you won't have to worry about them getting food stains on them. You can put them right back on after the meal has ended without needing to get another clean outfit out of the closet.

All of these are important pieces of feeding development because it helps them connect with what is going in their mouth by touching and experiencing it on their hands. They quickly begin to associate food on their hand and their hand going into the mouth with self-feeding. The baby has a sense of control by exploring the food with their hands, which helps to make the mealtime comfortable. Babies can recognize when they are full, and will eventually become adept at letting you know by turning their head away from the spoon, or pushing the spoon away when another bite is offered.

The next step in typical feeding development is where the baby will learn how to hold a cracker and eat it. This should be a simple transition where babies naturally pick up a cracker when offered, and almost reflexively bring it to their mouths. They should know what to do with it by now, because they have made a connection between food on their hand and eating or feeding themselves. Now the baby will learn to take bites off of the cracker and chew until the dry solid turns into a wet mushy texture before swallowing. The messiness continues during this stage where the baby gets the wet mushy texture often mixed with the dry solid crumbs on their hands and face while trying to eat the food.

I want to emphasize this point because as infants we consume a liquid (formula or breast milk), then pureed food (or baby food), which remain constant once we put them in our mouth. However, the cracker is the beginning of a more complex system where the food starts out one way, and ends up breaking down into a different form as we chew it. To be more specific, the cracker is dry to start, and turns into a wet ball of food (also called a bolus) which sticks together in our mouths as we chew and swallow it. This is very different from other foods like ground beef for example which spreads apart and moves all around in our mouth when we chew it. This is more difficult for little ones to manage, but with practice, they eventually become good at it.

Moving on through development, as babies become toddlers they begin to move from finger feeding themselves to also using a fork and spoon to feed themselves. The toddlers at this point will often attempt to use the fork or spoon, but will also revert back to using their fingers if they are not getting the food in fast enough or easily enough. I have seen this a lot with spaghetti, macaroni and cheese, peas, and many other foods. This is a typical and appropriate thing for toddlers to do. In fact, it also shows some problem solving skills!

I can think of an example where adults may do this as well. Think about the first time you tried eating with chopsticks. It was probably interesting to try for the first few minutes or bites, but unless you are a natural somehow, most likely you switched back to using a fork to eat the rest of the meal (and probably the majority of the meal). This is a skill that often takes a long time to master unless you practice using chopsticks with every meal that you eat.

In my practice, I have experienced many parents who get frustrated when their toddler uses their hands during meals once they have learned how to use a spoon or fork. I wanted to make this point: Toddlers will continue to use their fingers for a while even after they start using a spoon or fork. This is the time where you will see a child holding a spoon in one hand, but picking up food and eating it with their other hand. Looking at the chopsticks example, where adults resort back to the easier way of eating, it makes sense that toddlers would do the same thing.

In general, the parents who want their child to use a fork or spoon instead of their hands are the same ones who prevent the child from getting their hands messy as a baby. Often times, the reason for this is not because the parent is hyper about messes, but more likely because they do not like to get their own hands messy. In this situation, they are essentially protecting their baby from the "yucky" feeling of the food on their hands. The problem with this is that the baby may not think it feels yucky to begin with, but they learn from their parents reaction and decide that maybe it does feel yucky after all. This is one of the reasons why I stress letting the babies and toddlers experience the messes from the beginning! If they are not allowed to get messy, it could carry through the rest of their lives. The cycle could continue with their own children later in life.

This strategy continues as toddlers continue to practice using a fork and spoon to eat a larger and larger variety of foods. Another skill that develops along the same time as this, is being able to manage having a variety of foods and textures in your mouth at once. For example, dipping French fries (a solid food) in ketchup (a liquid) and eating them together in one bite. Most people don't think about this much, but it does teach the toddlers how to handle a liquid and solid in their mouth at the same time. Both of these textures move around in your mouth in different ways and toddlers are able to learn how to safely chew and swallow them together.

In addition to what is going on in their mouths, these toddlers are often getting the ketchup on their hands when dipping the French fries. Without thinking, they will usually just end up licking the ketchup off of their hands, and continue eating. This is still considered a typical stage of development. However, at this point a typical child should be eating a large variety of foods. They should be able to eat the same things as the rest of the family is eating for meals. Therefore, if you want to start teaching your child how to use a napkin to wipe their hands, it should not affect their continued progress. I would encourage you to offer a napkin if you want to, but also understand that your child is still going to lick food off their hands, and that is acceptable too!

I want to note here that those same kids that don't like getting their hands messy, will usually become very skilled, very quickly at using a spoon and fork. They are quick to figure out that if they use these utensils, there will be even less of a chance of them getting any food on their hands. Naturally, their parents will be proud of this also because of how great it is that their child learned to use the spoon and fork so well. While this is a great skill to learn, they don't understand that in this case, it is also reinforcing to the child that they don't have to get messy. Therefore, they won't have the natural repeated exposure to getting their hands messy which could lead to continued sensitivity as they continue to grow into adulthood.

Chapter 2: Tactile Sensory Processing

If I am going to convince you to let your kids touch their food I need to explain Tactile Sensory Processing. As an Occupational Therapist, I know that Sensory Processing is a major factor in the way we respond, react to, and understand the world around us. Each person has his or her own way of processing sensory information.

When the word "processing" is used in this way, I am talking about the way a person's brain receives information, thinks about the information, then responds or reacts to the information. An example of this is: Touching your finger in hot water, your brain thinking the water is "too hot", and responding or reacting by pulling your hand away from the hot water.

In this chapter, I will use examples that may be over-simplified or over- generalized for the sake of getting the point across to those people who are not familiar with this subject.

Tactile Sensory Processing specifically refers to how our brains process the things that touch our skin anywhere on our bodies. However, for the purpose of this book, I will mainly refer to how our brains process the things that get on our hands, fingers, arms, face, and mouth.

Keep in mind that one of the first ways infants learn to explore things in the world is by using their hands. They reach for their parents' faces, toys, rattles, their own feet, the bottle or breast, and many more objects in their environment. Infants explore these items by holding them and looking at them from all different angles. As soon as possible, infants begin to bring all of these things to their mouths for further exploration. At this moment, the relationship between the hands and the mouth becomes established. This means, that the child will explore items or food with their hands initially. Once they determine that the toys or food feel fine in their hands, they will test it out in their mouth. This is an extremely important skill!

Many parents prevent their baby from putting toys in their mouth. This can be detrimental to their baby's eating development well before they are eating pureed or solid foods. The hand and mouth connection is necessary for typical eating patterns and habits to develop. The bottom line is, you should allow your baby to use their hands to bring appropriate teething toys to their mouth for exploration!

In the next section, I will break down some of the ways we process Tactile Sensory Information. There are a few different ways of thinking about sensation. Some of the following information is based on ideas from Dunn's Model of Sensory Processing ("The Impact of Sensory Processing Abilities on the Daily Lives of Young Children and Families: A Conceptual Model").

The first example is where the child wants to have extra stimulation on their hands. Generally speaking, this child likes to have their hands messy. When they begin eating baby foods, they will likely reach for the jar or bowl of food with their hands. The food will end up all over their hands and face, and they will be wearing the biggest smile you've ever seen. As this child continues to progress through the stages of self-feeding, they will dig into the food with their hands and squeeze it in their fingers as much as possible. However, it is usually the case that children who crave tactile sensation will enjoy eating a large variety of foods. It is unlikely that these children would have any sensory-related feeding aversions. These kids actually love to eat, and often look forward to mealtime.

Going back to the relationship between our hands and mouths, these children love to touch and play with food; therefore, they love to eat foods with a variety of textures and flavors. Children who fall into this category will frequently want to eat "high sensory" foods (spicy, crunchy, sour, chewy, etc.). They like these types of foods because they get the sensations their mouths are looking for. To explain this in terms of processing: The food touches their mouth; the brain determines that it likes the texture and flavor, so they continue to chew and swallow the food. Then, they will repeat this action because the previous bite was so enjoyable!

The second example is where it takes longer than we would expect for the child to realize there is something touching their hands and face. They will often have food on their face or hands during and after meals and not realize it's there because they don't feel it. In other words, their brain doesn't realize that it feels anything on their skin. When you wipe their face clean, they usually don't resist. In fact, this can be one strategy for helping them become aware that they have food on their face.

In this example, the child will often use their hands to play and explore in their food. However, they are not doing this because they are craving the sensation and they can't get enough of it. In-fact, they may be touching the food for quite a long time before they even realize how the food feels or even that they can feel it at all.

As with the the first example, children in this section will also like to eat high sensory foods. I will often hear parents comment on how they are surprised that the child would want to eat things that are so spicy (like salsa or salt and vinegar potato chips). In this instance, the child likes the high sensory foods because it takes more sensations or stimulation for them to detect the flavors and textures in their mouth.

To explain this from a processing point of view: The food touches their mouth, the brain takes a while to detect the food in their mouth, the brain finally realizes there is food in their mouth, they chew (sometimes minimally) and swallow the food. They continue to eat more because they are hungry, and if the food has a lot of flavor or crunch to it, they usually like to eat it. I have seen many children that will take bites of a soft, bland food such as mashed potatoes, and continue to fill up their mouth until it is stuffed full. This is one instance where the food has very little texture or flavor to it, so they continue to fill up their mouth until they have the sensation that it is finally full. At that point, it is difficult to swallow because they have over stuffed their mouth, and choking is a concern. These children benefit from additional stimulation prior to and during mealtimes. Some examples might include offering a vibrating toothbrush or teether dipped in ice cold water to mouth on while waiting for the meal to be ready. These kinds of activities can help to get the child's mouth ready for chewing and eating foods safely.

The next example is where a child becomes very upset when any food gets on their hands. This is because they do not like the way foods (and other things) feel on their hands and face. This child will often prefer to eat finger foods consisting of dry textures that will not stick to their hands and fingers. If the food starts out dry like a graham cracker, and becomes wet and sticky as they eat it, the child will put it down and not want to eat that one anymore. They will also want to have their hands cleaned immediately, and will become upset if they are not wiped off fast enough. Depending on how upset they have become at this point, they may not want to eat anymore regardless of whether or not they are still hungry.

In this example, when the child gets food or sauces (like ketchup) on their hands, they will want their parents to wipe it off rather than just licking the food off themselves and continuing to eat more. In fact, the parents of these children will often tell me, "They don't like to eat Ketchup or Ranch Dressing even with French fries or chicken nuggets". The reason for that is the child has learned that by eating these sauces, their hands may accidentally touch it and that will not feel good to them. It most likely has nothing to do with how the sauces actually taste, but more to do with how it feels when it gets on their hands and face. They also may not like how it feels in their mouth.

These children will often get upset by the food being on their faces, but they may also get upset when you are wiping their faces clean. They don't want the food to be on their face, but they don't like the feeling of the washcloth touching their face either. Many parents are often confused by this. From the child's perspective, neither are good options. For one, if the food is on their face and they don't like the way it feels they get upset because they don't want it there. However, they don't like the way the washcloth feels when their parent touches it to their face to clean the food off. The parents usually understand that their child does not like the food on their face, but can't see why they don't want to have it wiped off. Both of these actions are related to sensory processing! It can be very stressful for both the parent and the child to get them cleaned up.

The children in this example will often learn how to use a spoon or fork earlier than usual. They are motivated to figure out these utensils because they won't have to touch any of their foods and risk getting messy. It is also common for these children to eat a limited variety of foods. They quickly become comfortable with a few of the beginning solid foods that are typically offered to kids, and they just stick with those because they have become familiar and predictable. These children will also often eat one texture of food at a time. For example, they will eat a chicken nugget, then they will eat a piece of cheese, and so on. They often resist eating foods that have a mixture of textures like spaghetti with meat sauce, cereal with milk, soups, etc. This is largely because early on they resisted eating foods with sauces to keep their hands from getting messy. Therefore, they did not learn how to handle eating mixed textures in their mouths.

The hand and mouth relationship with these kids starts at infancy. They will often initially attempt to use their hands for exploration, but quickly become upset by the way it feels. They learn to avoid touching the certain foods that make them upset. These children learn it is safe to explore certain foods with their hands, although they often only explore minimally because it is not always a comfortable activity for them. They figure out that the foods that feel ok on their hands also feel ok in their mouths. However, they also figure out that the foods that feel "bad" or "yucky" on their hands are not going to feel good in their mouth either. Therefore, they won't eat those foods.

When looking at this from a processing point of view there are a couple of ways to explain this. One scenario: The child picks up the food (wet/saucy) with their hands, the brain determines that it feels bad, and the child puts the food down and wants their hands to be cleaned up. Another scenario: The child picks up the food (dry) with their hands, the brain determines that it feels ok, they put the food in their mouth, the brain determines that it still feels ok, they chew and swallow the food, and continue on with another bite cautiously. In a final scenario, the child looks at the food, their brain determines that the food will feel bad if they touch it, the child picks up a fork and gets food on it, they put the food in their mouth, and the brain either determines that it feels ok in their mouth (so they chew and swallow the food; or the brain determines that it feels bad in their mouth and they gag on it or just spit it back out). These children figure out very quickly that if the food looks wet or saucy, they don't want it. This can be tricky and often becomes confused with the next situation.

The final example for this discussion is when the child is resistant to touching things that will get their hands messy. Another way of looking at it is that the child will resist or refuse to touch anything that looks like it will not feel good to them. For example, some children will not like to touch things that are wet, while others will not like to touch things only based on the fear that it is also going to feel bad to them. In actuality, other things may not feel bad to them at all.

To look at this from a processing viewpoint: The child looks at the food, their brain determines that it won't feel good on their hands and mouth, so they avoid touching and eating it. Another way to look at it is: The child looks at the food, their brain decides it does not look like it will feel yucky, they pick up the food and put it in their mouth cautiously, their brain determines that it still feels ok in their mouth, so they chew and swallow and continue eating."

The children in this example may initially start out looking like they fall under the previous example. However, the key is, in this one they *think* they won't like the way the sensations feel, whereas in the previous example, they actually do not like the way it feels on their skin. These children will avoid touching the food, which often also means they will avoid putting the food in their mouth for eating.

This can be a little tricky, because these kids will touch some foods with their hands. At first glance, it may look like there is no issue with touching different things. However, with closer observation, it becomes clear that there is a pattern in which types of foods or sensations they will avoid touching and eating. It is also possible that sometimes these kids will fall under both examples.

The type of foods that these children will eat varies per child, and depends on what each individual perceives is going to feel ok. They will often be very "neat" eaters so they can get through a meal without getting food on their hands or face. Many times, the children will eat a limited variety of foods, but the parents are proud that they are still clean when they finish their meals. In this situation, the child gets praised for not getting messy, which essentially reinforces the idea that it is ok to avoid touching the foods.

The hand and mouth relationship in this situation is often underdeveloped. The child may touch something and then discover they don't like the way it feels. Then, they will remember this one time and will associate it with other foods that look similar to the one they didn't like. The child will often avoid the new food because there is something about it that reminds them of the one they know they didn't like to touch.

This is often confusing for parents because they may not know all of these thoughts that are going on inside their child's head. Parents often don't understand that the child thinks the food is going to feel "bad" or "yucky" based on a prior experience. The child may not like touching certain things, and it affects their ability to touch new

things only based on the fear that it is also going to feel "bad" to them. When in actuality, other things may not feel bad to them at all.

One of the big questions is, "What causes this?" The exact cause of Sensory Processing Disorder is unknown, however, we know that certain people are at risk for having Tactile Sensory Processing difficulties. It is not uncommon to see this with children who have special needs. We often see these issues with children who have the following diagnoses: Prematurity, Autism Spectrum Disorder, Down Syndrome, Low Muscle Tone, Developmental Delay, Sensory Processing Disorder, Anxiety Disorder, and others.

However, the issues with tactile sensation can also be present in children without any diagnosis. One example of this is with infants who live or have lived in an environment where they do not have a lot of physical contact with their parent or caregiver. This has been known to happen in some orphanages around the world. Children who are considered "typically developing" and who come from a typical environment can also have difficulties with tactile sensation for unknown reasons.

Regardless of whether or not a child has a diagnosis, we need to address the issues with tactile sensation when it affects a child's ability to eat. It is important to eat a variety of foods in order to give our bodies the nutrients and vitamins we need to survive and to be healthy. This is especially important for children who are still growing and developing.

Chapter 3: Current Trends of Eating Skills:

In my practice, I have worked with many children and their families who struggle when it comes to mealtimes. The children that I work with have a known disability or delay, which has resulted in them qualifying for therapy services. However, being the skilled observer I am trained to be, I have come to realize that there are many typically developing children and their families in our culture that also struggle at mealtimes. I have observed this struggle many times at restaurants and other public places.

As I mentioned in the Introduction of this book, there seems to be an expectation that kids will only eat meat and cheese tacos. I can't think of one reason why a typically developing four year old should have a taco without lettuce and tomatoes! Many waiters and waitresses at Mexican style restaurants have been conditioned by our society to say, "meat and cheese only?" when we order a taco for a child. This is often presented as more of a statement than a question. While this may not seem like a big deal, this is just one very common example of what is going on in our culture. I have to wonder if this is a result of a child who is unable to manage a variety of textures in their mouth at one time, or if this is a result of learned behavior in a typically developing child.

I agree that we need to make accommodations for our children at mealtimes based on their skill level with chewing and managing different foods. However, it is important to offer them the same foods the rest of the family is eating at meals whenever possible. The young child may need to have portions of their meal pureed, diced, or cut up to appropriate sizes for their individual level. Or, using tacos as an example, the child may have the meat, cheese, lettuce, and tomatoes on their plate with a tortilla or hard shell as a side item. The child can practice eating all of these ingredients using a spoon, fork, or their fingers depending on their skill level with utensils.

I encourage parents whenever I can to get out of the habit (better yet, don't start in the first place) of fixing one thing for their child and something different for themselves. This practice suggests to children that the food their parents are eating is not going to taste good to them. The child figures that the food they are eating must be better than what their parents are eating. Thus, setting the stage for the child expecting to have something different from everyone else at meals. Parents will eventually get tired of preparing two meals at every mealtime, but the child has come to expect their special food because of what their parents have taught them. They may resist trying foods they don't usually eat because they assume if it's something that their parents eat, they are not going to like it.

Another trend I have observed surrounding mealtimes is the lack of expectation that children will sit down and eat. This example goes a few different ways. One example is that the parents will sit down for dinner, and ask their child, "do you want to eat?" This sets the stage for the child to say, "no." If the child says, "no," the parent should accept that as their answer. If the parents accept the answer as "no," the child will not participate in mealtime with the rest of the family. The child will often eat at a later time, and will typically end up eating something different than the rest of the family.

If a parent is going to allow their child to have a choice, the parent needs to respect the child's choice. However, many times, the parents will say, "Well, you are going to eat anyway." In this case, the parent has created a battle that never needed to be there in the first place. It is hit or miss how much the child will eat during this meal simply out of spite for thinking they had a choice, when they actually did not. When children are younger, people don't seem to notice this being a problem most of the time especially at the home environment. However, it gradually becomes a bigger and bigger battle as the child starts getting older. With younger children, it is usually not perceived as a problem until the family goes out to eat at a restaurant. It is difficult to get these children to sit at the table and "behave" because they are not expected to do this at the other mealtimes in their home. They may not understand why they are expected to sit and eat with everyone else at the restaurant.

The ideal situation would be to turn back time, and do things differently next time. Family mealtimes are where the whole family is expected to be sitting at the table, and eating the same type foods (appropriate consistency for their ages). If the routine is set up this way from the time the child starts eating in their high chair, these battles will not exist. The child will know this is the routine of mealtime, and they will not think there are any other options. However, since it is not possible to turn back time yet, the solution to this may be difficult especially in the beginning. Parents will stop asking the question, "Do you want to eat?" and start telling the child that, "we will be eating dinner in 5 minutes."

I would suggest having the child help with setting up the table for dinner in whatever way is appropriate for their age or developmental level. They can put silverware, napkins, ketchup, etc on the table for you so they have some involvement in the mealtime preparation process. Parents will need to explain that this is the time to eat (breakfast, lunch, or dinner) and we will not be making any other foods later. If you offer a snack later, that is ok, but it should not be a full meal where you cook or prepare another "dinner." Simply offer a few apple slices, carrot sticks, crackers, etc. I would also suggest that you refrain from allowing the child to have snacks before an upcoming mealtime especially in the beginning process. This will help them feel hungry and want to eat on schedule with everyone else. If they can't make it to the meal without eating some type of snack, again offer a fruit or vegetable that would supplement the upcoming mealtime but not allow them to get full before the meal. Keep in mind, this particular recommendation is for typically developing children who are at the appropriate height and weight for their age.

My background and experience has taught me to understand that young children often attempt to show their independence during mealtimes because they learn that this is one thing they have control over. This is a typical and acceptable stage for a child to go through. However, it does not let parents off the hook for being consistent and maintaining some ground rules during meals. It is not an excuse to let the child get their way with how meals are going to work. If the parent's expectations are practiced from the beginning this stage will most likely go rather smoothly. For those families who have not established expectations with eating, this stage can potentially lead to some difficult mealtimes.

# Chapter 4: Food Play Therapy

Early intervention is extremely critical for children with tactile sensory processing difficulties. This means starting sensory therapy with an Occupational Therapist as early as possible in order to have the best chance of success in changing the child's eating patterns. To begin with, parents will want to have their child evaluated by a licensed Occupational Therapist. This may be done at a local children's hospital on an outpatient basis with an early intervention program through your state. Or, you can find a therapist in your area that provides home therapy. It is preferable to have a therapist come to your home where they can observe your child in their own environment. Sensory therapy is most successful when the child's family is involved. When therapy is provided at home there is likely to be more consistency, which often results in faster progress.

It would be best to start therapy before the child turns three years old. However, if the child is older than three it does not mean it's too late! It is typically better to start earlier because the children's brains are still rapidly developing, and it is usually easier to get them to change. However, it is possible to have success with children older than age three as well. It may take longer before you see results from therapy, but it can happen if parents are patient and consistent.

Sensory therapy is extremely individualized. The Occupational Therapist will evaluate and make a sensory diet or sensory plan that is appropriate for your child. In the following section I will discuss general tactile sensory therapy techniques and ideas. However, these are generalizations, and will not work for every child. I recommend that you discuss these ideas with your child's Occupational Therapist to ensure they don't interfere with their sensory plan.

Tactile sensory therapy can generally be broken down into two main categories: **"Tactile Desensitization"**, and **"Tactile Awareness."**

Tactile desensitization can be further broken down in two ways: how sensation actually feels, and how the child thinks the sensation is going to feel. First I will discuss tactile desensitization with regard to the child who does not like the way things (specifically foods) feel on their hands. This is the child that does not like how sensations feel on their skin. The technique that is often used with these children is exposure therapy. Once it has been determined what specific sensations the child does not like to touch, a plan can be made for how to start exposing them to these sensations. Basically, this is going to help establish the hand to mouth relationship in a new way.

Generally speaking, therapy will consist of playing with food. The food play should be done at a time before a meal or snack when the child may feel slightly hungry. The point of food play at this time is to get them comfortable with touching a variety of foods and textures. However, if the child is hungry they may be interested in tasting some of the foods on their own. If they want to taste the foods that would be great, but it is not something that should be pushed.

It is also a good idea to set them up at a play table or some other area rather than where they usually eat snacks and meals. For some children, when placed at their meal table, they immediately begin to have negative feelings. This can prevent them from participating in the food play at all. However, there are also children who actually do well sitting in their high chair or at the dinner table for food play therapy. Sometimes, they do better this way, because they can make the connection easier between touching the food and eating it.

The decision of where to have them participate in the food play should be decided based on what their comfort level is with the meal table or high chair. There are some children who are most comfortable standing next to a table, sitting on the floor, or even being outside for food playtime. These are accommodations that should be allowed depending on the child's needs.

When is comes to the food play activity, it should be as creative and as fun as possible. There are so many different ways to play with food that they cannot possibly all be listed! Some examples include: using carrot sticks as cars that "drive through a pudding racetrack," using ketchup to paint a Spiderman picture, stacking up apple slices to make a big tower, making handprints using grape jelly, and millions of other ideas. The best thing to do is look at the child's specific interests and use those as a starting point. The next step is being creative and finding ways to incorporate their interests into the play activity using the appropriate foods.

The play activity will involve the child and adult. The adult is expected to play with the food and be a model for the child. The child will be more likely to want to participate in the playtime if their parent appears to be having fun doing it! If their parent refuses to touch the food and get involved, the child will often not want to do it either.

It can take some time before the child will be willing to touch the food and get involved in the activity even with the parent participating. However, the child cannot be forced or pushed into touching the foods. Forcing them to do it will only cause more resistance and negative feelings towards the situation. Often times, the initial sessions will result in touching the food incidentally if at all. The child may want to mostly watch the parent play at first which is a good start. If they decide to participate in the play, the child may accidentally get some of the messy food on their hand. If or when this happens it is important to not make a big fuss about it.

Depending on the individual child, it may be best to act like you didn't notice it and continue playing as if you didn't see it happen, or calmly tell them "good job" for touching it, and allow them to wipe it off. Then, take your attention back away from the "issue" and continue on with the food play as before. The child will often judge their parents reactions and copy them. Therefore, if the parent remains calm and relaxed, it may help the child not get as upset as they usually get in that type of situation. These types of activities are highly individualized to each child. An experienced therapist can help guide you through the appropriate levels of food play therapy.

The idea behind this is that the more the child has exposure to foods, the more familiar the foods become to the child. Over time, they begin to realize that they can experience the food textures, and they will still be ok afterwards. This can take quite a long time depending on how well the child responds to the food play, and how well the food play activity is presented to the child. However, once the child starts to touch foods in play, they are often able to start touching new foods with less and less hesitation over time. This is especially true if the food play process is handled in an appropriate manner for that child.

As the food play activity progresses, the child will be encouraged in an indirect manner to smell, touch the food to their face or mouth, lick, etc. As I said before, the child will not be forced to do this! They will be encouraged to try if they want, and the parent will be smelling, tasting, licking or whatever else the child is being encouraged to do. These children may still feel sensitivities to touching things, but they learn to deal with the way the textures feel. They also learn that they can touch them, and they may feel slightly uncomfortable with the feeling for a short time. However, once they are done touching the food textures they will feel fine again, and the uncomfortable feeling will be gone. This type of play will help them figure out how to cope with the feelings and be able to experience a variety of foods to touch and hopefully eat.

In a second example, of Tactile desensitization, a child *thinks* they don't like the way a food feels. This child may have had an early negative experience with touching a food, and now they associate that negative experience or feeling with touching other foods. Once they do finally touch the food or texture on their hands, they start to realize that it actually doesn't feel too bad to them after all.

Once they figure this out, they replace the negative experience and feelings with positive experiences and feelings. The child becomes more willing to touch a variety of food textures.

Some children will even start to look forward to experiencing different foods. This positive experience also leads to more positive feelings surrounding tasting and eating a larger variety of foods and textures as well. The child makes the association that the food feels ok on their hands so it will probably feel ok in their mouth as well.

The other type of tactile sensory therapy I would consider tactile awareness. This type of therapy is used with children who either take longer than we would expect for them to realize the sensation is there, or for kids who really want more sensations and like the stimulation from the foods and textures.

For children who take longer to recognize sensations, Tactile Awareness is when the child touches foods and textures using their hands in order to become aware of what their hands are doing. For these children, therapy involves using foods that have a lot of texture (ex: bumpy, crumbly, rough, squishy, etc) because touching the textures will help them be able to process the feeling of the foods on their hands faster.

The child will be encouraged to squeeze, smash, poke, squish, and more using their fingers and hands. Generally speaking, children in this example are willing to touch the foods and play in this manner. The feeling of the textures does not bother them. In fact, they may not realize when some of the food during the play activity gets on their forearm or even on their face.

Another strategy with these children for tactile awareness is to offer high sensory foods for them to eat. These "high sensory" foods typically include spicy, crunchy, chewy, sour, gritty, or cold textures. By offering these bold textures and flavors it helps "wake up" their mouths so they can feel what is going on in there. This helps the child be aware of their lips, teeth, tongue, etc so they can take in food chew and swallow safely.

At mealtime, it is common to offer one of these types of foods early in order to prepare their mouth for eating. The meal itself may consist of high sensory and low sensory foods. However, if the meal does not have a high sensory food, the child should definitely experience some type of tactile awareness prior to eating. For example, stimulating their mouth with a vibrating toothbrush, facial massage, using sour spray or drops of lemon juice, or pieces of crushed ice.

There are many reasons why tactile awareness play may be necessary for these kids. Some of the issues with feeding or eating that may be present include holding and using a spoon or fork, getting the food into their mouth using their hands and utensils, difficulty with chewing foods or not chewing foods at all, swallowing issues, difficulty with learning to drink from an open cup or through a straw, etc. These are all possible results of not being able to register or feel what is going on with their hands and mouth, which can lead to problems with eating.

From a processing perspective: the child brushes their teeth using a vibrating toothbrush, their mouth feels stimulated, they take a bite of food, their brain determines that the food is in their mouth, so they chew and swallow the food appropriately. On the other hand, if the child does not have the tactile stimulation prior to eating, the child takes a bite of food, but their brain does not determine that the food is in their mouth right away. In this case, they may close their mouth and hold the food in the front of their mouth for a while. When their brain finally realizes the food is in their mouth, they either chew a few times and swallow or just swallow without chewing.

The other kids that may benefit from tactile awareness are those kids that are wanting more stimulation. For this style, the strategies are the same but the reasoning behind them and the effects are different. These are children that will enjoy playing with foods and textures using their hands. They will often find ways to purposefully get into these types of activities without prompting from an adult. These children will often love eating a variety of foods, and will often enjoy mealtimes very much. They are usually good at chewing foods, and prefer to eat foods that require a lot of chewing like meats, chips, and fresh fruits and vegetables.

This is because their body (mouth) enjoys the way it feels to have these sensations stimulating them. A simple way to think of it is that the child feels jittery or "wired." When they are able to squeeze, smash, chew, or crunch foods it provides a calming feeling in their body. These children also seem to enjoy getting messy because they like the way the textures feel on their hands and face. It is not likely they will get upset when they are messy. However, they may not resist having their hands and face wiped with a washrag because they like the way it feels when it rubs on their skin. Washing them off may be pointless because they will most likely get back into the messy activity if it is still available!

From a processing standpoint: the child takes a bite of food, their brain immediately detects the food in their mouth, they begin chewing right away and chew as long as they can, then swallow the food, and repeat the activity without needing encouragement.

Although the focus of this book is Tactile Sensory Processing with eating, I need to mention Oral Sensory Processing as well. The Oral Sensory area includes your face, lips, mouth, teeth, and tongue. As I mentioned earlier, children typically develop a hand-to-mouth connection through early play and exploration with toys and food. If this connection is not established, children may also display difficulties in processing not only tactile sensations on their hands but also oral sensations in and around their mouth. The treatment for this often begins with treating the tactile sensation of the hands first. Often, when children begin to tolerate sensations on their hands, they also begin to tolerate them in their mouths as well.

However, I am not suggesting that you should ignore the oral area and focus only on the tactile area of the hands. It is important to begin working with the child's oral sensory needs at the same time as starting to work with the tactile sensory needs of their hands.

The Oral Sensory area is often the same as the Tactile Sensory area in each individual. What I mean by this is that children will often either have a sensitivity to both areas or will take longer to feel the sensations in both areas. Just like with anything else, though, this is not the case one hundred percent of the time.

There are instances where the oral area takes longer to realize the food is there, and at the same time, the child doesn't like the way certain things feel on their hands. The ideas for working with each area are the same. Desensitization strategies are used for kids who don't like the way things feel in their mouth, and awareness strategies are used for kids who don't mind the way things feel, but take longer to notice the foods that are in their mouth.

The process for desensitization of the oral area often starts with activities that involve stimulation to the face, chin, cheeks, and lips areas.    This might include things like touching different textured items (clothing, washcloths, and other materials) on their face and mouth area. Repetition of exposure to a variety of items over time can be very helpful in this situation. Using vibration on their hands, then moving up along their arm to their shoulder and side of their face to where they are eventually touching it to their lips is another strategy you can try. This process of getting from their hands up to their face and lips can take a long time, and possibly even several different trial sessions before they start to get comfortable with it. Of course, it could take even longer for some kids to get there and that's ok too.

After this stage, you might move on to some messy food activities where the foods start to get on their cheek, face, lips, etc. These activities should be part of food play therapy that is ideally monitored by their Occupational Therapist. From there you might move on to various stages of getting the food on their tongue, teeth, or inside of their cheeks. These activities will gradually and eventually lead to biting and chewing foods, and ultimately swallowing them! This is often a very sensitive process, and I would highly recommend following the lead of your Occupational Therapist to ensure the strategies are appropriate for your individual child.

Oral desensitization can potentially take a long time to occur with children. Again, as all children are different; some take longer than others to adapt and make changes towards accepting foods. It can be a frustrating time for parents because we want our children to start eating better right away. However, it is important to approach this therapy with patience and understanding. Your child's Occupational Therapist should be able to help you see the slight changes or improvements along the way.

On the other hand, Tactile Awareness strategies are often easier to do with kids who need it. These are children who don't have any trouble with touching the foods and getting their hands messy, therefore, they may be more willing to put foods in their mouth. However, the tricky part is usually helping them realize the food is in their mouth and now they need to do something with it!

This is again due to the processing where it takes longer for their body and brain to realize that they feel something in their mouth. One strategy to keep in mind is using what we call "high sensory" foods to bring awareness to their mouth or to "wake up" their mouth. Some examples of high sensory foods are things that are crunchy, chewy, spicy, sour, cold, sweet, and bitter textures and flavors. Things like salt and vinegar flavored chips, ice chips, lemon juice, cinnamon spice, and beef jerky, are just a few examples. The actual foods that you might use will be different based on the individual chewing, swallowing, and other general eating abilities of the child.

This may also be a good time to try using chewy tubes or vibration activities like a vibrating toothbrush to help stimulate their mouth and prepare their mouth for eating foods. The chewing on the chewy tubes and the vibration are both good choices for trying to wake up the mouth area, and make them more aware of what is going on there.

Most of the time, children who are unaware of the sensations in and around their mouth, really tend to enjoy vibration. They will often love to bring a vibrating toothbrush for example, to their face and place it in their mouth also. They may not try to actually brush their teeth as we think of using toothbrushes. However, they may just bite down on it with their teeth or just hold it in one place in their mouth.

This is stimulating their mouth and making them more aware of that area which includes their lips, tongue, teeth, and cheeks. They will literally start to process the sensations and start realizing they can feel their mouth in that moment and probably for a short time after they stop using the vibration. This is an excellent time to work on eating skills like tongue movements and chewing food using the molars.

You can also use a mirror so the child can watch and see what they are doing. You can work on having them imitate moving their tongue side to side or sticking it out, or touching the roof of their mouth with the tip of their tongue. These all depend on their developmental skill level and age. They can practice chewing skills using a chewy tube or different types of foods where they use their molars to bite and chew it. These are all important skills for safe eating to decrease the risk of choking and gagging.

Children with decreased awareness often hold food in their cheeks for hours or longer. The child may not realize it is there because they can't feel it, or they don't know how to get it out of their cheeks using their tongue. They might also know that they have trouble chewing that food item, and want to avoid bringing it towards the middle of their mouth because they are afraid of potentially choking on it. I have heard many stories from parents about how they found food in their child's cheek hours after they were done eating that particular food. They had no idea it was even in there until they accidentally discovered it somehow during the day.

# Chapter 5: Other Senses Involved In Eating

While this book is focused on the tactile processes of eating, the Tactile Sense is not the only area of sensation that plays a role in how and what kids eat. Of course, humans are complicated creatures, so we cannot simply break eating down into a tactile activity alone. We use all of our senses to determine whether we want to eat certain foods, and whether or not we like certain foods. At this point in time, we understand that humans have many senses that affect our daily lives. We have the familiar 5 senses that everyone learns which are: Taste, Sight, Hearing, Smell, and Touch. In addition to the main 5 senses that we all know about, I will discuss three other senses that have become more well known and discussed in recent years: Vestibular, Proprioception, and Interoception.

Our sense of taste is also called the Gustatory System. This is where we process the way things taste. Each individual has a unique Gustatory System which explains why some people like foods that other people do not like. Generally speaking, our taste receptors, called taste buds, are located on the tongue and in the roof of the mouth. Once the taste buds receive stimulation by touching a food item, our bodies begin to process what that item tastes like by sending the information to the brain. The brain processes the taste(s) and sends signals back to the tongue/mouth once it determines what the next step will be. Typical next steps might include either eating or not eating the food item. For example, the individual may decide the flavor is a preferable one, so they continue taking the food into the mouth and eating it. On the opposite side, the individual may decide they do not like the flavor, and they will remove the food item instead of eating it.

We can look at this sense by relating it to the different ares of sensory processing. Children who take longer than others to notice tactile sensations and those children who want more of the sensations may like the foods that have higher flavors. Some examples may include foods that are: Spicy, salty, sour, bitter, minty, cinnamon, tangy, etc. We may also use cold (thermal), crunchy, and chewy foods as a way to provide additional stimulation to their mouth.

From an Occupational Therapy eating / feeding standpoint, the Gustatory System may be considered a second step in gathering tactile sensory information. As discussed earlier, children often begin by exploring foods using their hands (Tactile sense) and move on to bringing the food to their mouth for the next step of physical exploration. The Gustatory System is a process for sensing taste. This is how we determine the flavors of the food that we eat. The inside of the mouth is also a continuation of the Tactile System. Not only do we taste the food item that is placed there, but we also feel the texture of the food. We can determine whether the food is crunchy, soft, chewy, one single texture like cheese, a mixture of textures as in a bite of pizza, and so on.

We also determine whether the food stays together to form a ball (or bolus) of food or whether it spreads out into multiple areas. For example, bread often forms a bolus of food when you chew it, whereas, spaghetti with meat sauce spreads out when you chew it. These are not concepts we typically think of when we have typical sensory processing systems. However, for children who are sensitive to or who need additional tactile stimulation, these are very important concepts to consider.

Children usually don't have the communication skills needed to tell you what they like or don't like about foods. For example, children who are sensitive to tactile stimulation are more likely to spit food back out once it touches their mouth rather than explain to you that they don't like the way the food feels in their mouth. From the opposite standpoint, children who need additional tactile stimulation may put too much food in (over-stuffing) before they begin to actually feel (or register) the food stimulus.

Since we are unable to rely on children to explain why they like or don't like certain foods, we have to become very good at observing and piecing together all of the information surrounding their individual sensory processing systems.

The sense of Sight often plays a role in mealtimes with children who are sensitive to textures on their hands and in their mouths. They will use their vision to inspect the food before deciding if they want to touch it and bringing it to their mouth. Some children will be ok with picking the food up, then look at it more closely by turning it over in their hand before taking the bite. On the other hand, they may look at the food and decide they do not like the way it looks, and they refuse to pick up and taste it.

Sometimes, as parents we offer a bite of food to our children either from our hand, fork, or spoon. The child who simply does not like the way things feel on their hands will take a look at the food offered, and either try a bite or turn away based on how the food looks. If there is anything that looks different or questionable to them, they will notice it and will turn it down most of the time. It is not a good idea to try and sneak food in with their preferred foods because they will notice either before or after taking the bite. This can destroy a trusting relationship between parent and child, and that trust is very difficult to rebuild! It could also make them suspicious of all foods, including the foods they typically prefer which could end up limiting their food intake even more.

The next sense to discuss is the sense of Hearing. In the sensory world we call this "Auditory Processing". This refers to the way our brain processes what we hear, not whether or not we CAN hear. How can this affect eating and mealtime? Some children have Auditory Processing difficulties where they get distracted by noises in their environment. They are unable to block out the sounds in their environment that are unimportant such as fans, people talking in the room, music or tv sounds, and more. The inability to block out background noises means that their brains are trying to process ALL sounds in the room! This is impossible to do, and often ends up causing the children to feel anxious and upset because they become overstimulated.

This can affect a child with tactile issues because if they are feeling overstimulated, they are less likely to want to try a new or non-preferred food. They will most likely want to stick with foods that are familiar, and ones that they are used to eating. It could also be the case that the child may not want to eat at all for that moment in time. Even foods that are preferred or familiar may not sound appealing. Think about a time when you were nervous or anxious about something. You get that feeling of butterflies in your stomach, and the last thing you feel is hungry! That is partially due to the adrenaline that comes with anxiety or stressful situations also. But, in this case, it probably has to do with the adrenaline plus the overall sensory overstimulation that's going on with them.

In the next sense, which is the sense of Smell or Olfactory sense, we are processing the variety of scents or smells in the environment. Sometimes the foods that are presented to us have a scent, and that scent may be pleasing or it could be obnoxious. Each person has their own likes and dislikes when it comes to the sense of smell, much like the other senses!

In terms of processing, we basically either process the smells really quickly or there is a delay in the processing. So, for those who process the smells quickly, they are not only processing fast but also potentially processing every smell in the room or around their area. This is the person who can smell or detect every ingredient in a meal just by taking a quick whiff. This is also a person who might be on a walk, and smell the scent of a certain flower before you even get to it on the path.

This type of processing could either work to your benefit or it could become problematic. If the person smells everything and is ok with the smells, they will likely be a person who enjoys eating foods and experiencing new flavors. However, a person who is not ok with all of the smells may become easily overwhelmed and actually feel somewhat nauseated. This can make a person not want to eat anything, and they might be a person who gags at the smell of certain foods.

Of course, foods aren't the only thing in our environment that smell. A person who is sensitive to smells will not only be potentially bothered by the smells of foods, but also by things like air fresheners, candles, lotions, and soaps. The smell of their own clothing could be bothering them if they were freshly laundered or if they used a new detergent to wash them.

A child in this situation would likely prefer foods that are more bland, or that don't have much of a scent to them. Those types of foods will be less likely to elicit a gag reflex with these children because they may be less stimulating to their sense of smell.

On the opposite side of this, is a person who has a delay in processing the smells around them. Their nose might breathe in the smell and send the signal to their brain, but their brain has a slower reaction time to realizing what they smelled or even that they smelled something at all.

In this case, the person will be less likely to resist foods, but they might actually prefer foods that have a higher flavor or scent! This way, the child will have a better chance of detecting the scent of the food and it may help them become more interested in eating the foods and actually enjoying them.

The next sense is the sense of Touch or Tactile Sensory processing which I have already talked about in great length in previous chapters. So, I won't get into it again here, other than to reiterate that it is the way we process things that we touch (on our skin and in our mouth). Some people are more sensitive to touching things than others, and some people want to touch things even more than others!

Now, in getting to the three additional senses that I wanted to mention for this topic. First, I want to talk about the Vestibular sense. This is the sense that is detected by the semi-circular canals in our inner ears. Those canals have fluid in them that moves when we move. It is the way that we detect which way our head is in space. It lets us know if our head is up, down, sideways, and if it is spinning, jumping, sitting still, or moving in any direction at all.

You may be wondering what this has to do with a child eating. Well, some kids will feel the need to get more movement. These are kids that seem like they never sit still! They like to run, jump, spin, and generally keep moving all the time. Those kids who are doing this because of a sensory processing need, are trying to get more stimulation of their head and therefore body. It can be difficult for these kiddos to sit still long enough to sit in their chair and get through a meal. They may feel the need to get up and wander around in the middle of the meal, or stand up in their chair a lot, or get down on the floor and spin in circles. There are so many possibilities.

We need to find ways for these children to get their vestibular needs met either before or during the meals so they can sit with the family and eat their food without getting up and moving around. They may benefit from some intense movement activities for about 20 minutes before the meal starts. Maybe they go through a routine of jumping on the trampoline, then spinning in an office chair, then doing somersaults across the room. Then, possibly repeating these activities a few times (like circuit training). These may not be the three activities that each child should be encouraged to do, these are only some examples of possibilities.

The idea here is not to "wear them out," but to help them get their head moving in different ways that stimulate their vestibular system. Therefore, getting the need met and allowing them a brief opportunity afterwards to sit and eat their meal before feeling the need to get up and move again.

For those kids that don't respond to moving around like this, they could try using a balance disk or a therapy ball to sit on during meals. This will allow them to move while sitting by wiggling back and forth in their seat but not actually getting up.

Another area of sensory processing is Proprioception. This is the sense that determines where your body is in space. This is detected by the muscles, joints, and tendons in your body. To some people this can look similar to the Vestibular sense, and frequently kids who have needs in one area will actually have the same needs in the other area also. But, they are two different things.

Kids who have Proprioceptive needs are ones that might run into things a lot. They might bump into the wall or the couch when walking past them. They might trip and fall frequently, and seem to trip over invisible lines on the ground. The child who has issues in this area, might have trouble determining how much force to use on an object. For example, they might slam the door to the house really hard each time they close it because they are unable to regulate how much or little force to use on the door to get it closed.

This child may also be interested in moving a lot, but the proprioceptive reasons for moving are to feel their body crash on the ground or on cushions, or to roll around on the floor to feel their body on all sides. These activities are considered deep pressure activities. They give the child a sense of where their body is in this world. By feeling the pressure of other objects on their body, they can determine literally where they are standing, sitting, laying, etc.

This can affect children with eating, because they may have a difficult time keeping their body in an upright position to stay in their chair for the meal. They need to have the extra stimulation in order to determine how to keep their body in the seat. It's not only important for being able to keep their body in the chair, but also for how much force to use when picking up their food either with their hands or using their utensils.

A child who is struggling with these things might benefit from doing some deep pressure activities prior to sitting in their chair for meals. Similar to the vestibular activities, this may not be quite enough to get them through the whole meal. So, they may also benefit from using weighted lap pad or heavy item that they can hold in their lap during the meal. You could try wrapping a thera-band around the legs of their chair, so they can kick the thera-band and stretch it with their feet and legs for resistance during the meal.

They might also be fine with simply placing a foot stool under their feet so they can have a stable surface to give them a sense of where their body is. When they are too short to reach their feet to the floor, their feet might just be hanging in the air. The foot stool can give them a better sense of security and just basic understanding of where they are so they don't feel like they are floating in the air.

The final sense I wanted to mention is Interoception. This is the sense of what is going on inside our bodies. Interoception is how we determine things like whether or not we are hungry and thirsty, if we need to use the bathroom, if our stomach hurts, or if we have a sore throat.

You can imagine this is important for when it comes to meals and eating because if the child doesn't detect that they are hungry, they may be less likely to want to eat. There will be less motivation to eat foods if they don't feel hungry, and then if they don't feel full and satisfied after finishing the meal. The same goes for being thirsty and wanting to drink enough fluids to maintain hydration.

A child who has difficulty with this area might confuse feelings of hunger in their stomach with a stomach ache. As a parent, we may think the child is complaining of a stomach ache meaning pain that is associated with an illness or other gastrointestinal issue like constipation. In reality, they might simply just need to eat some food, and that "stomach ache" will go away because it was from hunger rather than actual pain. It can be difficult for a child with these difficulties to determine what is really going on within their own body and communicate that to their parents in an effective manner.

Another way this could affect kids is if they eat and feel full right away (because their body is so sensitive to the feeling of food in their tummy). They might not want to eat a whole meal because their body is telling them they are full after only a few bites or a small portion. On the opposite side of this, their body may not recognize the feelings in the stomach at all, and this could make them keep eating too much because they don't feel the full sensation. The child may finally feel "full" once they have over-eaten and now possibly not feel good because they ate too much!

In either case, parents need to be aware of what is going on so they can find ways to help their child eat an appropriate amount of food for each meal. On one hand, a child could be at risk for not gaining enough weight, and on the other hand, they might be at risk for becoming over-weight. The strategies for these kids will vary depending on each individual child's needs, and you should consult your child's Occupational Therapist and possibly also a Nutritionist for a specific plan of action.

Chapter 6: Considerations for Children with Special Needs:

Why do some children have tactile sensory processing difficulties? At this point in time, there is not one particular cause for any type of sensory processing differences. The way people process sensation is different from one individual to the next.

For some children, the way they process sensation is passed down from one or both of their parents. This can be helpful at times because the parent understands from their own experiences how their child feels when they touch messy foods. However, this can also make things difficult when I am working with the parent on how to begin Tactile Desensitization with their child. The parent may also have a difficult time getting their own hands messy because they do not like the way it feels either!

In other cases, children have differences in processing because of environmental factors. For example, they are not allowed to get messy so their parent wipes their hands immediately when something gets on them. This sends the message to the child that getting messy is "bad" or "yucky." In other examples, the opportunities may not be there for children to experience foods and textures due to financial difficulties or cultural beliefs. For some parents it can be considered wasteful when their child plays with their food rather than looking at it as an important method of exploration.

Sometimes children have sensory processing issues and there is no known or obvious explanation. It can be common for kids who have a medical diagnosis or some other type of developmental diagnosis to have issues with sensory processing.

It is not a problem to have different sensory processing abilities because, as I already mentioned, each person has their own way of processing sensation. However, it becomes a problem when it interferes with our ability to function and take part in daily life. Parents will often begin to seek help for specific things like getting their child to eat, sleep, learn new things, communicate, play with toys, socialize with others, etc. It is only after an Early Interventionist gets involved that parents often become aware that the underlying cause of their difficulties may be due to sensory processing.

In this book, the main focus has been on Tactile Sensory Processing. I did briefly discuss some of the other senses, although not in as much detail as the Tactile sense. Of course, all of our senses can affect a child's ability to eat. As a therapist, I look at all of these when working with a family to ensure that we are setting up appropriate strategies for each child based on their individual needs. There are so many variations on how children process all of the sensations, it would be nearly impossible to discuss them here in detail.

It is not uncommon to see Tactile sensory processing differences in children with special needs. In fact, it should always be considered as a possibility when evaluating a child for early intervention. Having a medical diagnosis does not automatically guarantee there will be issues with sensory processing. However, it should always be considered as part of the evaluation process in children with and without a diagnosis. Children with Cerebral Palsy, Down Syndrome, Autism, Prematurity, and many other medical diagnoses have been known to experience differences with Tactile Sensory Processing. There are also many children without any medical diagnosis that have difficulties with sensory processing.

For example, with children who have Cerebral Palsy, a therapist would evaluate how they process sensation on their skin in general. Children with Cerebral Palsy often have loss of motor function affecting one or both sides of their body. It is not uncommon for children with this diagnosis to have differences in sensation in the same places that the loss of motor function occurs. Sensation with these children can vary depending on the type and severity of the brain damage that occurred to cause the Cerebral Palsy.

Children with Down Syndrome may also experience some differences with tactile sensory processing. A common strategy for meal and food choices with these children might include "high sensory" foods such as crunchy textures, and spicy, sour, or bitter flavors. It is not uncommon for children with Down Syndrome to need stronger flavors in their mouth in order to taste food due to their sensory needs. These types of foods can also help "wake up" their mouths for chewing because of the increased sensation the textures and flavors provide. Children with Down Syndrome can also have low muscle tone throughout their body. This often affects mealtimes when you are trying to teach the child to finger feed themselves.

Some children have difficulty with picking up the food from their high chair tray due to motor delays, Tactile Sensitivity (with touching a variety of textures), or a combination of the two. Some strategies for this include having the child "wake up" their hands before meals by squeezing play dough or other squishy toys, playing with their hands in a box of dried beans or rice, or pounding a toy with a hammer and pegs. These types of activities may help stimulate their hands so they may have an easier time picking up their food and bringing it to their mouth.

Children with Autism and children who were born prematurely are also at a higher risk for having tactile sensory processing issues. With these two diagnoses it is difficult to predict which type of issues they might have with sensory processing. Children with these diagnoses could have sensitivities or crave additional sensations, and these could change from day to day. So, I won't get into more details about each of those for the purpose of this book. I just wanted to mention that sensory issues can be common in children with these diagnoses so you will be aware of it as a possibility.

# Conclusion

I want to end this book by summarizing some of the important factors to consider when working with your toddler on eating skills. For one, not all issues surrounding feeding and eating skills are related to Sensory Processing. There are many other reasons out there why a child may have issues or difficulty with eating. However, for the purpose of this book, the focus was on eating difficulties due to Tactile Sensory Processing issues.

If you suspect or know that your child has issues with sensory processing or other developmental concerns, please seek an evaluation by a qualified early intervention professional in your area.

The information and activities discussed in this book are intended for parents to gain more of an understanding of the way sensory processing works, and how it can and often does affect children's abilities to eat. It is not intended to take the place of early intervention therapy, but rather to supplement the information your child's therapist is already providing to you.

# References

Dunn, W. (1997). The Impact of Sensory Processing Abilities on Daily Lives of Young Children and Families: A Conceptual Model. *Infants and Young Children*, 9(4).